The Quiet Soul

Practices for Finding Everyday Connection to Your True Self

By Ann Biese & Laura Stein

Art by Colleen Sgroi

For Laura Du Pont Stein (Dupe), my best friend of fifty years, for teaching me how to speak kindness to my own heart and to listen to my Quiet Soul. There is no greater gift in the world.

And for my dad who taught me that nature can bring you quiet joy.

AB

To Ann Key Biese who I have been blessed to call my best friend through all of these years. Thank you for your support and understanding and for always believing in me. Everyone deserves an Annie in their life!

And to my mom and dad, thank you for introducing golf into my life which instilled in me the need to listen to my instincts, to recover after a bad shot and to play my own game.

LS

PUBLISHER'S NOTE

This book is designed to provide helpful information on the subjects discussed and is not meant to be used for taking the place of diagnosing or treating any medical condition. The ideas and suggestions contained in this book are not intended to be a substitute for consulting with your physician. Neither the publisher nor the authors are engaged in professional advice or services to the reader nor shall they be liable for information suggested in this book.

Copyright © 2023 DEK Publishing
Illustration Copyright © 2023 Colleen Sgroi

All rights reserved

No part of this book may be used or reproduced, stored in a retrieval system or by any means including photocopying, recording, scanning without written permission from the author or publisher under the 1976 United States copyright act.

Printed in USA

Cover Art by Colleen Sgroi
Book Design by CS Creative Services

ISBN: 9798852346308

Library of Congress Control in Publication on file with Publisher

Contents

Introduction

True Connection

Soul Self

Best Friend

Quiet Soul

Final Thoughts

Introduction

THE JOURNEY TO BECOMING YOUR OWN BEST FRIEND

Today is the day I begin to speak kindness to my own heart.

Ann Biese

The intention behind creating this journal is very simple. I want to share a new life path that I have taken and demonstrate how it has helped me create a self-love for my own happiness and well-being that I never realized I could have. I am truly more at peace and have a much deeper understanding with my own heart. I began speaking to myself as my best friend speaks to me! This self-love journey has brought a new energy for everyday living unlike anything I could have ever imagined.

A life transformation commonly comes about as a result of a complete emotional breakdown. Case in point: I had just started a new profession and was trying to navigate a family move while recovering from a surgery. In a moment of rushing and trying to do it all, I accidentally locked our family dogs in my car outside the coffee house while the realtor's showing our home. I called myself an idiot; tears began to stream down my face.

I was completely overwhelmed, tired and thinking I do not manage my life well. I was at complete surrender! After a car service arrived and unlocked my car, I got in and drove home thinking the entire time that I need to do better. The self-scolding was repeatedly voiced in my mind. I called my best friend with full-on tears, and her words to me were, "Annie, that's a lot. You are totally doing too much. Give yourself a break." And there it was, a sense of kindness and compassion, a sense of wisdom, and a sense of understanding.

So, how did I begin this journey to become my own Best Friend? I sat on my back deck feeling the warm sunshine on my back. I closed my eyes for a moment of peace, and I thought "I need to talk to myself like my best friend does." In that Quiet Soul moment, I made a vow to try and treat myself as my best friend would.

We invite you to embark on this journey of self-realization joy and inner peace. Books are typically read from start to finish. The lessons in this book can be completed in sequential order or any order you choose. This is your journey... forge your own path.

True Connection

When you begin each day by asking yourself "What really matters to my heart?" you are already living your life with true connection.

Before you get out of bed, place your hand on your heart, and take few deep breaths. Then, remind yourself ...

I matter to me.

Draw a heart on this page, and write inside
the things that matter to you.

Did you know that spiders don't get stuck in their own webs? Unlike spiders, we can get stuck in our own web of thoughts. So often, our mind is spinning and keeping us from discovering a true connection with who we really are.

In this web write ways in which you can begin a true connection with yourself.

Make a list of ways you can begin to run in the direction of your heart.

- _____
  _____
- _____
  _____
- _____
  _____
- _____
  _____
- _____
  _____
- _____
  _____
- _____
  _____
- _____
  _____
- _____
  _____

"To Be, or Not to Be? That is the Question"
William Shakespeare

In Shakespeare's play, Hamlet, the quote above was a question about human existence. Although it was quoted hundreds of years ago, I like to think about it in modern times. We have become increasingly distracted by digital devices, to a large extent smart phones, that we no longer take in the moments of being present in our own lives.

How much of our time has become "Not to be?"

Reflect on a time that you felt so alive and in the moment. What did it feel like "TO BE"?

_____
_____
_____
_____
_____
_____
_____
_____
_____
_____
_____
_____
_____
_____
_____
_____
_____
_____

It is in the roots, not the branches that a tree's greatest strength lies.

Matshona Dhiwayo

True connection to the strength of who we are lies in the roots of our character.

Write in the roots of this tree the qualities you know to be true about you.

heartfelt

in American English

('haːrt, felt)

ADJECTIVE

deeply or sincerely felt

Word origin

(1725-35; HEART+FELT) Collins Dictionary

Everyone has experiences that touch them deeply and sincerely, but living a heartfelt life has challenges too.

Journal on the next page about a time you really did not want to work through a heartfelt life challenge. How has it helped you grow?

I Choose to be True to ME!

We need to be consciously aware that we have a choice in all matters, especially relating to our truth.

Take a reflective moment and think of three positive words you can say to yourself daily.

Write those three words in the circles below.

I choose to be true to me, myself & I!

A One Minute Reflection of Me.

Take one minute to simply breathe naturally right now wherever you are. Notice the inhale. Notice the exhale. When you focus on your breathing, your nervous system begins to discover a connection with your true self, and it activates natural healing to your mind and body.

Take a moment and write what it felt like to spend time with your true self.

_____
_____
_____
_____
_____
_____
_____
_____
_____
_____
_____
_____
_____
_____
_____
_____
_____

A whole person connection with your soul self is a journey that you can continuously build on in life with your own spirit.

Soul Self

S Something
O Out of this world
U Uniquely
L Light-Hearted

On this page, write about something
"out of this world" that you would like your
soul self to accomplish in this lifetime.

S
O
U
L

You do not need to take a million steps to begin a journey with your soul self. Truly, it may take only a few steps down a guided path.

This week, jot down on several post-it notes when you recognize the steps you need to take to align with your soul self journey.

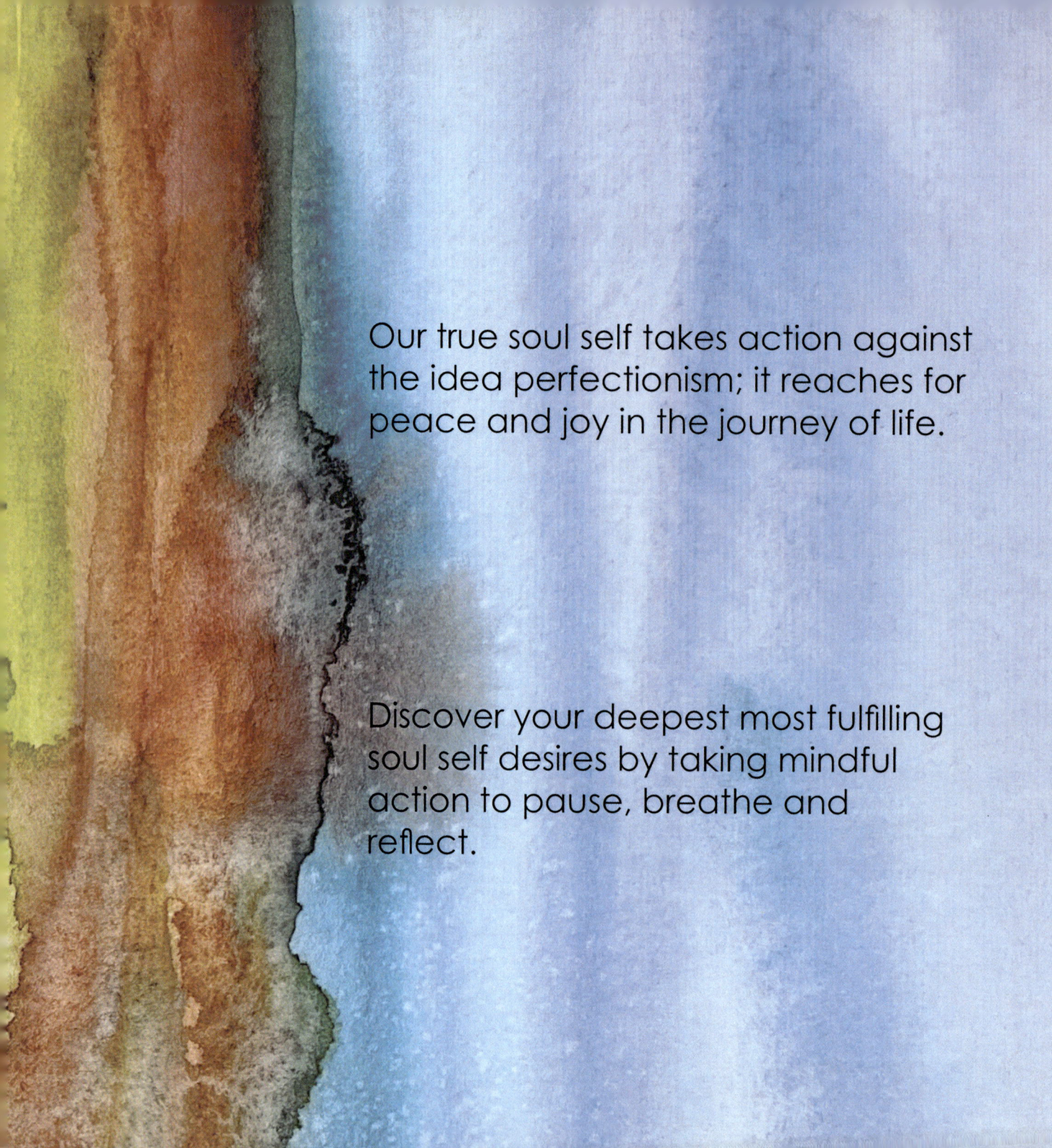

Our true soul self takes action against the idea perfectionism; it reaches for peace and joy in the journey of life.

Discover your deepest most fulfilling soul self desires by taking mindful action to pause, breathe and reflect.

The fire in your soul needs its flame for true transformation.

Ann Biese

Our journey to work and live with our soul self needs tending just as a fire does; we do not want our flame of life to fan out.

On this page write about a way you can reignite your flame through this journey of the Quiet Soul.

If we want true connection to our soul self, we need to be willing to spend time in quiet reflection.

SOUL

vs

MIND

Take the *7 minute, 7 day Meditation Challenge.*

Here is a path to action.

Bee kind to your mind and sit with your soul self.
Put an X on the bee of every day you sit in meditation.

The contemplative shift of your soul self happens when you sit with your Quiet Soul.

Now, after sitting in meditation for a week, share on the opposite page about your experience. Be honest, and allow the journey to be worth all your efforts.

Laughter is a sunbeam of the soul.

Thomas Mann

Nothing can be more therapeutic than laughing with our soul self. Studies show that laughter lowers blood pressure, burns calories and can improve our mood for days.

On the following page, write about some laughable moments you recently enjoyed.

What are some ways that you can take action to be connected with your soul self?

On the next page, use the 4 R's model to reflect on your intentions.

 To Be Rejoicing

 To Be Reflective

 To Be Responsive

 To Be Renewed

A One Minute

Reflection of my Soul Self.

Take one minute to simply breathe naturally right now where you are. Notice the inhale. Notice the exhale. When you focus on your breath, your nervous system begins to discover a connection to your soul self and it activates natural healing to your mind and body.

Write what it felt like to reflect and spend time with your soul self.

_____
_____
_____
_____
_____
_____
_____
_____
_____
_____
_____
_____
_____
_____
_____
_____
_____
_____

Best Friend

What Is Friendship?

The poem, *A Reason, A Season or A Lifetime* was written by an unknown author but has been attributed to Eleanor Roosevelt and Brian A."Drew" Chalker. It begins, "People come into your life for a reason, a season, or a lifetime."

Think about the friendships you have had in your lifetime. Who has been a friend for a reason? A friend for a season? A friend for a lifetime?

We may have one best friend or many close friends that we include in our circle of trust. We might develop these friendships over time by common interests or experiences. While we refer to you being your own best friend, this may look different for you than for others. Let all of your friendships help guide you to a better relationship with yourself - a guide to being your own best friend.

Write the name(s) of friends in the spaces below.

A Reason

_____
_____
_____

A Season

_____
_____
_____

A Lifetime

_____
_____
_____

The Impact of Family & Friendship

> Some people arrive and make such a beautiful impact on your life, you can barely remember what life was like without them.
>
> Anna Taylor

Family - As we are born into this world, we don't have a choice when it comes to the family we grow up with. Our family experiences can leave us feeling loved or perhaps not so loved. Ultimately, if we are fortunate, family members can also become friends.

Friends - Our friendships, on the other hand, are formed completely by choice. Friendships can develop deliberately or by chance, but how deeply and long-lasting those friendships evolve are always a choice.

Impact - Interactions with our family and with our friends influence how we look at the world, what we value, what beliefs we hold and who we become.

Circle the group below that has had the most impact
on who you have become.

If you would answer both almost equally, circle both. Then,
below each group, write "**+**" if that overall impact was positive,
and "**-**" if that overall impact was negative.

        Family   Friends

Express your thoughts about why you answered the way you
did and describe any lessons you have learned from your
experiences.

_____
_____
_____
_____
_____
_____
_____
_____
_____

To Be Your Own Best Friend...Focus on Balance

The Merriam Dictionary defines balance of mind as: emotional equilibrium: sanity

While the concept may seem simple, balance is often difficult to achieve. We live in a world where we are always plugged in.

Keep this actonym in mind:

B — Begin with small steps

A — Admit your negative patterns/behaviors

L — Let yourself unwind

A — Always treat yourself with grace

N — Notice how you feel in the moment

C — Celebrate small victories

E — Expect it may be challenging

Almost everything will work again if you unplug it for a few minutes, including you.

Annie Lamott

If you are struggling with balance in your life, unplugging may support you in achieving better harmony. Here are a few ideas for you to try.

- If you are at work, take a walk during your lunchtime
- Drink more water during the day
- Meditate
- Run a diffuser with your favorite essential oil
- Prioritize sleep and turn off digital devices
- Arrange a bouquet of flowers for yourself
- Try to spend 15 minutes a day decluttering
- Read a book or listen to an audio book

Write a few extra of your own below:
_____
_____

When you find something that helps you balance your life come back to this page and add it to the list.

Good, better, best.
Never let it rest.
Until your good is better and
your better is best.

Tim Duncan

Life can be overwhelming. Best friends make our good better and our better best.

Think about tomorrow. What might be a way you can make it better?

Think about next month. What might be a way you can make it better?

Think about next year. What might be a way you can make it better?

You may have listed some ideas from your balance exercise, but if you would like to challenge yourself to think even deeper, come up with ideas that may push you out of your comfort zone. You are worth it!

Listen

Good friends are the people who know when to be quiet and listen or when to tell you the words you really, really need to hear.

Katrina Meyer

Life consists of silent, ongoing internal dialogues that we have with ourselves. Choose a day, and truthfully listen to some of the things you are saying to yourself.

Write down those dialogues that stand out to you.

Now, spend the time to write down what you really truly needed to hear.

My internal dialogue:

What I really truly needed to hear:

Listen Listen Listen Listen Listen
Listen Listen Listen Listen

Reflection On Friendship

Reflect upon what you appreciate about your friends. How do those people treat you that shows care and understanding?

Capture your thoughts below.

_____
_____
_____
_____

Rate yourself on a scale of 1 to 5

Thinking of your best friend,
rate yourself on a scale of 1 to 5.
I AM treating myself as my best friend treats me ...

1	2	3	4	5
I can do better		I'm halfway there		Totally!

How important is it that I treat myself as my own best friend?
___
___
___
___

What am I willing to change in order to be my own best friend?
___
___
___
___

How will I make that happen?
___
___
___
___
___

Friends are the people who make you smile brighter, laugh louder and live better.

Unknown

Having a sense of humor about yourself is a gift.
It is important not to take ourselves too seriously.

Our friends are some of the people we laugh the hardest with. Don't forget, laughter is medicine for the soul.

Reflect on the moments when you laughed really hard with a friend. Why were they funny to you?
Choose one or two words that represent each moment, and write them below.

_____
_____
_____
_____
_____
_____
_____
_____
_____
_____
_____
_____

Remember these words when you are taking yourself too seriously, and always remember to keep laughter in your heart.

A One Minute Reflection of being my own best friend.

Take one minute to simply breathe naturally right now where ever you are. Notice the inhale. Notice the exhale. When you focus on your breathing, your nervous system begins to discover a connection with your best friend self, and it activates natural healing to your mind and body.

Spend some time writing what it felt like to reflect and spend time with your best friend self.

_____
_____
_____
_____
_____
_____
_____
_____
_____
_____
_____
_____
_____
_____
_____
_____

Quiet Soul

Quiet the mind and
the soul will speak.

Ma Jaya Sati Bhagavati

Today is the day you can set aside a small amount of time for three quiet breaks. At each quiet break, write down something that you believe you can learn to love about having a Quiet Soul. As an example, you could sit outside and enjoy the day's weather.

Break #1
_____
_____
_____
_____

Break #2
_____
_____
_____
_____

Break #3
_____
_____
_____
_____

You spend the first part of your life
collecting things ...
and the second half getting rid of them.

Isabel Allenede

We collect possessions in life, but we can also collect things that are either positive or negative and relate to our identity, mind set, emotions and how we see ourselves as we navigate life. It is never too late to release the negative things that are getting in the way of us loving our Quiet Soul.

Take a few moments and write down on a slip(s) of paper those thoughts that you would like to release in order to increase your appreciation and love for your Quiet Soul.

Cut the slip(s) of paper into many pieces. Find a way to dispose of those pieces of paper and "get rid" of them. We suggest putting the slips of paper into the bottom of a flower pot or in your garden and planting seeds over the top. Let the new blooms serve as a reminder of your renewed love for your Quiet Soul!

Having a Quiet Soul doesn't necessarily mean we are a quiet person but means making time for quiet self-reflection and finding a few minutes a day to include a meditation practice. This exercise activates multiple parts of the brain.

Practice the SLOW DOWN technique of a quiet mind by sitting and touching hand to fingers ...

Sitting with and loving your Quiet Soul can sometimes feel like a lotus flower before it blooms. A lotus grows in muddy waters but emerges with beauty and strength.

Write words of encouragement and kindness on the lotus leaves to remind you that you too will emerge with beauty and resilience from the murky waters.

Peace

It doesn't mean to be in a place where there is no noise, trouble or hard work. It means to be in the midst of those things and still be calm in your own heart.

unknown

When you love your Quiet Soul, you can choose to walk with peace anytime. Talk a walk alone in nature. Pick up a simple piece of nature, a stick, a rock or a leaf. Observe what you see and feel.

Glue or tape on the page what you found on your peace walk and write why you picked this up.

Write down what your peaceful walk meant to you spiritually.
_____
_____
_____
_____
_____
_____

One day, she gave herself a little grace, and though it felt strange, she realized she needed to be her own best friend.

Ann Biese

I need to have my own back!

Sit and do a yoga pose called cowface arms. Place one hand on your heart and the other on your back.

Reflect on someone who always has your back.

Now repeat out loud, "I have my own back, and I am my own best friend."

A One Minute Reflection of Grace to me.

Take one minute to simply breathe naturally right now wherever you are. Notice the inhale. Notice the exhale. When you focus on your breathing, your nervous system begins to discover a connection to your gracious self and it activates natural healing to your mind and body.

Spend some time writing what it felt like to reflect and be gracious to yourself.

_____
_____
_____
_____
_____
_____
_____
_____
_____
_____
_____
_____
_____
_____
_____
_____
_____
_____

Final Thoughts

You've Got This!

Laura Stein

Once upon a time, there were two young girls, Annie and Dupe, who could never have imagined how much fun and pure joy they would experience by collaborating on a book based on finding connection to your true self and being your own best friend!

On my wedding day, the bridal party was leaving the hotel on our way to the church. It had been a busy morning getting ready and attending to the final details associated with any big celebration. As we passed by a McDonald's, Annie asked the limo driver to pull into the drive thru because the bride needed to eat! I had not thought to stop for lunch, but Annie knew what I needed. It was a long aisle and a hot summer day and she wanted to make sure I was at my best! As we exited the drive thru, one of the other bridesmaids yelled out, "We all need an Annie in our life!" We all laughed, and I was once again reminded of the incredible blessing of her friendship. A friendship that would continue to grow even stronger in the years that lie ahead.

When we finally had a chance to watch the wedding video and we reached the end of the ceremony, there was Annie in the distance, still at the front of the church with her bouquet raised high above her head. She cheered our walk back down the aisle as husband and wife with excitement, joy and love. Because I was facing the opposite direction I didn't see it in the moment, but it was just another example of how she had my back then and always.

We would like to extend our heartfelt gratitude to you for the time you have invested in reading and completing the lessons in this book. The importance of reflection, responsiveness, rejoicing and renewal in our lives can't be stressed enough. Revisit these lessons as many times as you would like to support your own growth and well-being.

We sincerely hope that you have gained a deeper connection and new perspective on your relationship with yourself and the importance of being your own best friend. Make sure to have your own back and remember we all need and deserve to be Annie in our own lives! You've got this!

Finally, a big thank you to Colleen Sgroi whose stunning artwork in this collaboration took our breath away!

WE ARE BEST FRIENDS.

ALWAYS REMEMBER THAT

IF YOU FALL, I WILL PICK YOU UP...

AFTER I FINISH LAUGHING.

unknown

Here Are More Ways to Experience The Quiet Soul

Start your very own discussion group.

Download our free Group Guide available at annbiese.com.

Join Us for a Quiet Soul Retreat! Email lstein@dreamvacations.com to find out about our upcoming schedule.